Fashion Drawing for Advertising

Patrick John Ireland

fashion
drawing
for advertising

B. T. Batsford Ltd, London

To Professor Albert Reimann
founder of the Reimann Schools
of Berlin and London

First published 1974
© Patrick John Ireland 1974

ISBN 0 7134 2820 1

Printed in Great Britain
The Anchor Press, Tiptree, Essex

Contents

Acknowledgments   5

Introduction   6
1 Figure drawing   10
2 Fashion drawing without a model   23
3 Fashion detail   44
4 Fashion reporting   52
5 Techniques, texture, pattern   56
6 Faces, hair styles and hats   76
7 Fashion images   88
8 Layout and presentation   98
Glossary   121
Materials   123

Acknowledgments
I would like to thank Nick Bate and Alan Hamp of Batsford for their generous help with some of the more technical aspects of this book. The staff of the library of the College of Fashion and Clothing Technology were always helpful in aiding my research. Finally, I would like to give thanks to Geraldine Fallon for her able typing of the book.
P.J.I.

Introduction

The Fashion Artist must have a complete understanding of fashion and its many facets. An awareness of current trends and the influences which shape them is vital, and is assisted by attending fashion collections, exhibitions of textiles and shows of women's, men's and children's wear. By studying the latest magazines, window displays and recent techniques in advertising the artist will be able to keep in tune with his subject.

The student should practise drawing from life, sketching from a model and constructing figures from the imagination. The careful study of the many different materials and the way in which they drape, etc., is important. It is helpful to have a certain understanding of the history of clothes and the way in which they are made-up; this knowledge will assist in producing convincing drawings of the designs which are illustrated. The development of techniques with the use of various media and experimentation with new styles of drawing, form part of the study. Equally important is the preparation of the work and an understanding of the techniques of reproduction used in magazines, books, newspapers, etc.

Some artists specialize in certain aspects of fashion; others work in a wider field. An appreciation of the many different areas in which one could be working is essential: newspapers, magazines, catalogues and display, etc. Each of these media require appropriate consideration of style and interpretation.

This book, it will be seen, has been divided into various chapters and the subjects have been arranged in separate areas for study. It will be noted that at the end of each chapter exercises are suggested.

It is essential to keep in touch with new methods of presentation and to note the current feeling in advertising, the lay-out and arrangements used to reflect a certain period or mood. By regular study of magazines and newspapers an assessment can be made of the current tendencies.

It is also helpful to make a study of the displays in shop windows, boutiques and department stores. The windows present, with imagination, the fashion of the day, promoting new colour combinations and accessories.

Through the careful observation of window displays of shops and department stores, with a high standard of display, it is possible to capture the feeling of a trend: the Twenties, Thirties or Forties in Hollywood, Military and Gipsy looks, etc.

The displays reflect current fashion and designs. They are promoting, by the use of window display models posed in the attitudes of today, with wigs and make-up that emphasise the style of the moment. The presentation is considered with care to reflect the policy adopted. It is an advantage to attend fashion shows whenever possible; many department stores stage shows at the beginning of each season.

The profession of a fashion artist offers many opportunities to attend shows, to visit wholesale collections, exhibitions and Couture Collections. When visiting shows observe particularly the way in which the clothes are presented, new attitudes, make-up technique and hair styles. Through constant observation and involving oneself in the world of fashion the artist will be able to produce drawings that reflect the current feeling.

1 Figure drawing

The study of Life drawing and a knowledge of anatomy is a great advantage. It is helpful to work from a fashion model. This is not always possible and often the fashion artist will have to produce drawings relying on imagination and a knowledge of the human figure.

Illustrated in this chapter are a number of techniques which could be of assistance when working without a model. In time, and with constant practice, you will develop methods of your own which suit your own particular style of working.

Sketch from life when possible figures in different attitudes, and so train your eye to observe detail and the characteristics of people in various situations. In fashion illustration it is permitted to exaggerate the figure proportions to put an idea over. For example if the current look for a certain fashion is emphasis on long legs this would then be reflected in a stylisation of the figure which places disproportionate emphasis on the legs (see illustration).

Basic figure proportions

The basic figure proportions are 7½ to 8 heads tall (see illustration).
The following stages illustrate how to construct the figure.

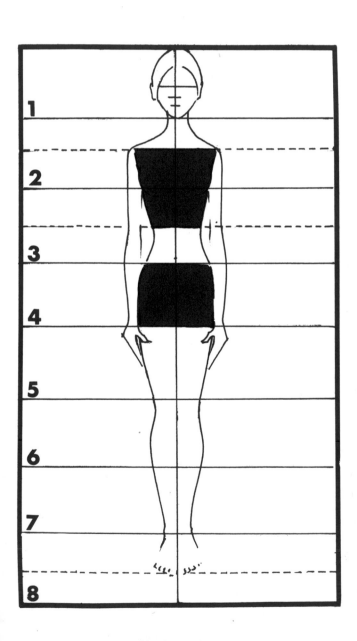

1. When constructing the figure measure off 8 spaces.

2. Sketch a vertical line through the sections, this will provide you with the centre front line of the figure.

3. Start the sketching of the figure with the oval shape of the head.

4. The shoulder line would be placed half way between number 1 and 2 line.

5. Divide 2 and 3 in half, this will provide the waist-line. The pelvis and rib cage have been suggested in the two solid shapes.

6. Hand falls between 4 and 5.

7. The knee cap comes between 5 and 6.

8. Line 7 the ankle.

9. Line 7 to 8 provides the heel and position of the foot.

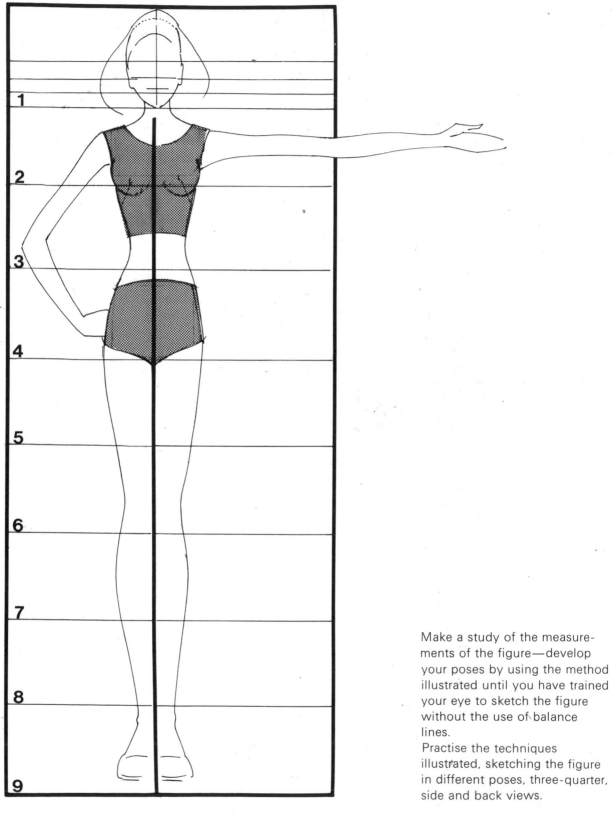

Make a study of the measurements of the figure—develop your poses by using the method illustrated until you have trained your eye to sketch the figure without the use of balance lines.

Practise the techniques illustrated, sketching the figure in different poses, three-quarter, side and back views.

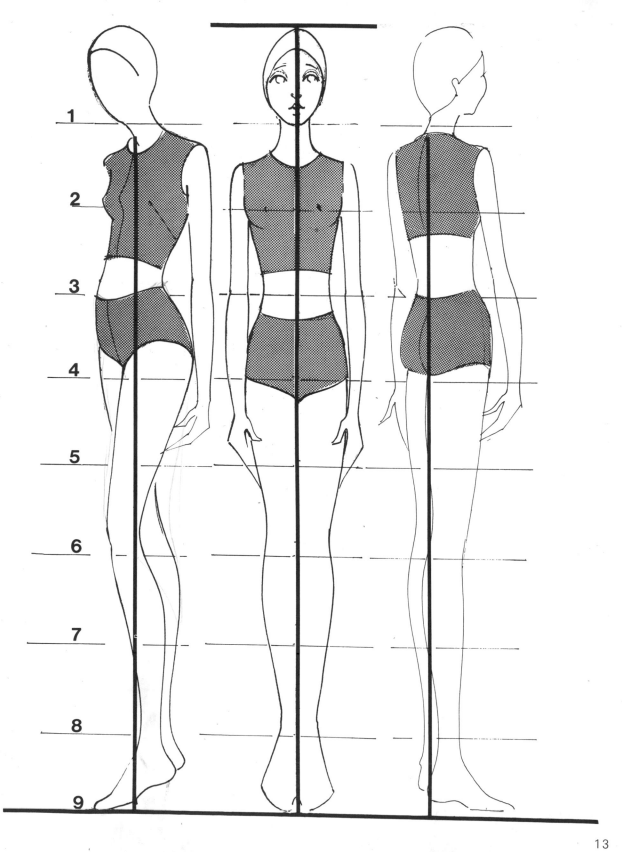

1

2

3

4

5

6

7

8

9

13

Note the swing action of the chest and pelvis when the weight is placed to one foot. The balance line supports the figure. This line, when correcting the figure, is always placed from the pit of the neck to the foot supporting the weight of the figure (see illustrations opposite).
Note the use of the centre front line when turning the figure and how the line curves according to the position.

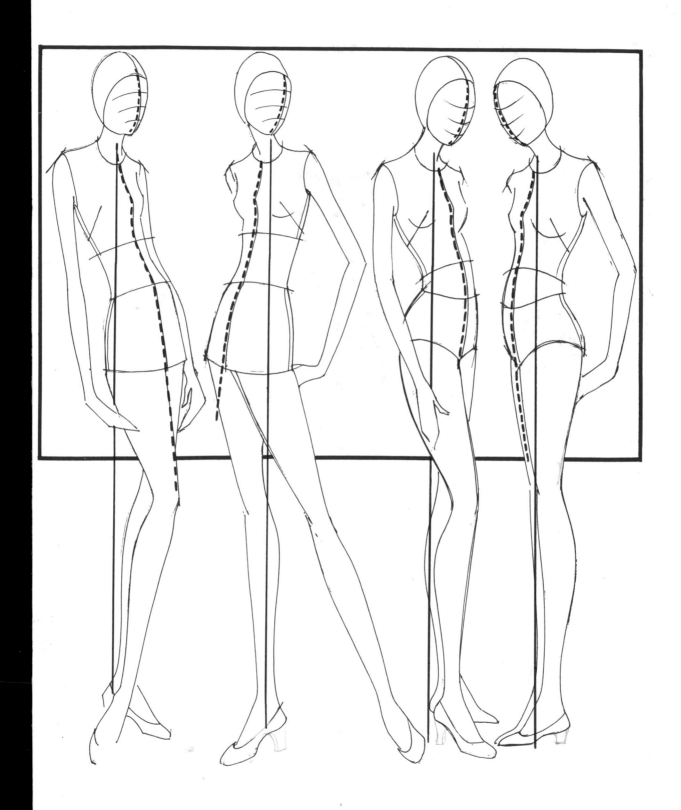

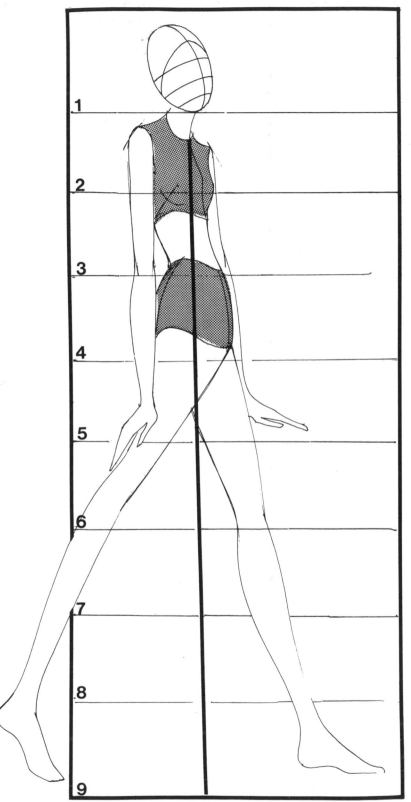

Figures in movement

Action poses may be required when illustrating ski-wear, swim suits and dancing etc.

It is very important to have some understanding of the activity you are illustrating. A careful observation should be made with quick sketches indicating different attitudes and movements.

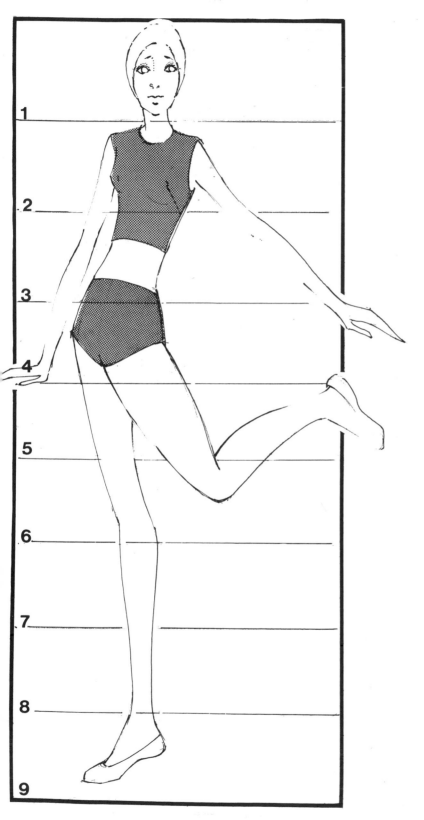

Develop new poses all the time that reflect a current feeling of fashion that would be suitable for different illustrations, i.e. Sports wear, Evening wear, Day wear etc.

Memory and observation

A well-trained memory and observation are very important to the fashion artist since conditions of work vary so considerably.

When working from a model in a wholesale showroom or fashion department in a store it is necessary to work at a certain speed so as to avoid keeping the model or the garment from the customer.

Observe, whenever you can, the details of garments and attitudes of people. Make quick sketches in your sketch book when attending the theatre, or any social event. However, if it is not possible at the time to make sketches, memorise what is possible and make sketches and notes later for future reference.

The following fashion images would each require a different approach in the drawing of the figure.

Romantic A graceful pose. The hairstyle, face and treatment of the dress express a romantic feeling. The proportions of the figure have not been unduly exaggerated.

Sporty Action pose full of swing and movement, note the emphasis on the legs and arms. Face has a happy expression with a carefree hair style.

Elegant Tall figure, emphasis on the length of the legs, graceful pose, placing of the feet and position of hands. Small head, long neck, facial expression distant and detached.

Develop a selection of poses, this will require constant practice. This technique could be of great assistance when developing poses without the aid of a model or photographic reference to work from.
Note the same pose with variations of the arm position. When developing your poses place a sheet of layout paper over your original sketch and work out different poses in this way.

Figure drawing

When developing varying techniques of figure drawing, experiment with different figure proportions until you achieve the Look and Image on which to illustrate the garment. It is important to reflect the correct type and pose related to the fashion you are illustrating. Often a number of poses would be developed before deciding on the most suitable (see illustrations).

2 Fashion drawing without a model

It is an advantage to be able to make fashion sketches without the use of a fashion model.

To do so is not easy for the beginner. You will need to practise with different methods of developing poses and constructing the figure and drawing the garments. You will find it helpful to keep a collection of fashion photographs of different poses and attitudes, listing them under such headings as 'Action poses', 'Elegant', 'Sporty', 'Dancing', etc. This can be a useful source of reference when working.

Always keep your collections up to date. Go through them and replace fashion photographs that you find are no longer suitable.

It is important to be able to draw the figure from imagination and to visualize it from different angles and in movement. The first stage would be to consider the most effective pose and angle to illustrate the garment to advantage. The pose selected should reflect the current mood and feeling.

The second stage will be to study the garment which is to be illustrated and to note the following: the basic shape of the garment, texture and pattern of the fabric, the way in which the fabric has been cut. The shape of the collar, type of sleeve and the placing of pockets, etc., are all highly relevant.

The third stage will be to experiment with different poses, constructing the figure from the imagination and using techniques illustrated. Start by making rough sketches of the garment at different angles and attitudes. Emphasize the important fashion features of the design, taking care that all the details are correct and in balance with the figure.

The final stage, when a number of rough sketches have been made, would be to select the one considered most suitable. Decide on the image you wish to project through the illustration: the design should suggest this. The final effects will be achieved by the technique used, whether pen and ink, brush, crayon, etc., and the type of model portrayed by the suggestion of face and the hair style and accessories that are shown (see illustrations).

Exercise:
Select a garment and make a sketch of it from the hanger. Imagine it as worn on a figure and make a drawing of it without a model, constructing the figure from imagination (as illustrated).

1. Study a garment, the cut, material, drape, dart placement and style details.

2. Decide on the image the fashion suggests, i.e. pose, type of face, hair style and accessories to complement the design.

3. Select the type of paper, (smooth, rough, etc.,) and the media to use, pen and ink, brush, crayon, etc.

4. Consider presentation and general effects.

25

Make rough sketches developing poses working with the methods illustrated, noting:

1. Heads into the figure and shape of head.

2. The balance line.

3. Centre front line following the movement of the body.

4. The position of the rib cage and hip position.

5. Length of arms and hand position.

6. Length of legs.

7. Position of the feet.

It is good practice to place a thin transparent sheet of paper over them and work over your roughs. Develop them, making alterations as required, leaving out the construction lines.
Make preliminary sketches, considering the pose and attitude of the model. Experiment with hair styles and facial expressions until you are satisfied with the final effects.

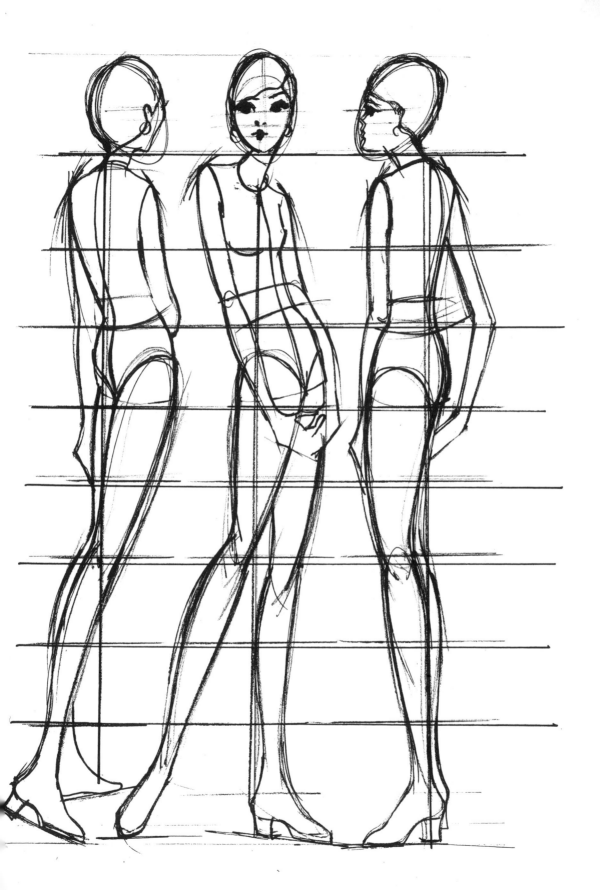

27

Make preliminary sketches, considering the pose and attitude of the model.

Select from the preliminary sketches the one you consider to be the most suitable for the final illustration.

Decide on the image to be projected, considering the type of face, hair style and accessories to complement the design.

Note the construction of the figures using the method illustrated.
Many poses may be created by this technique.

It is important to achieve the correct balance of detail, i.e. pockets, buttons, collars, etc. The drawings have been produced in pen and ink and the details painted in with white ink, the surface of the paper used was very smooth.

Teenage figures in casual wear. Note the awkward pose, windswept hair and position of feet. Make a number of sketches before deciding on the final one. The pose should express the mood of the garment being illustrated.

Note the simple construction of the figures illustrated and the way in which the coats have been drawn round the figures. Practise developing poses and retracing them using layout paper sketching the garment on the figure.

Stylized figure sketched in two stages; note how the figure has been constructed, indicated by the dotted line.

Three stages of producing this illustration of an evening suit and blouse.

1. The simple construction of the figure sketched from imagination.

2. Layout paper placed over the sketch of figure developing the garment round the pose, considering cut, texture, weight and drape of the material. Black designer's colour applied with a size eight brush has been used on smooth white paper.

3. Final effect with tint used for the silk blouse pattern and white paint for the details.

Developing a pose

When developing a pose without the use of a model it is helpful to use some sound construction lines to ensure the correct proportions and balance of the drawing. The following illustrations show the different stages:

1. Sketch the figure in with light pencil lines.

2. Design carefully round the figure, taking care to ensure the details are balanced (i.e. hem lines, etc.).

3. Note the centre-front line and balance line (or centre of gravity line) which drops from the pit of the neck, down to the foot, supporting the weight of the figure.

4. The pattern of the fabric has been indicated on one side of the figure only, giving the effect of light coming from the left side of the figure.

5. Hair style, necklace and shoes complement the design and suggest a young elegant look.

1. Rough outline sketch.

2. Sketch developed with shading and patterns.

3. The final illustration, re-traced from roughs and completed using tints and fibre-point pen.

When sketching children's fashion it is important to obtain the correct proportions according to the age and type of a child, also suggesting the type you are illustrating.

Collect good examples of photographs and illustrations by fashion artists taking note of the many different approaches to sketching children from very stylized work to a more realistic approach.

Study the attitudes of children. Make sketches and collect different poses—playing games, walking, running, etc. These sketches will be useful later for reference when illustrating children's clothes.

When developing the figure balance the figure from the centre front line, indicated by the dotted line.

Note the movement of the folds, of the skirt and sleeves also the pattern of the material suggested on one side of the figure, indicating light on the other.

Draw from life when possible, working with quick sketches, depicting the model from different angles, and using a free, loose line. The drawing could be developed depending on the effect required.

When you feel your work is beginning to become too rigid sketch from life and work out new techniques, experimenting with new pens, brushes, crayons, paints and papers.

Stylization

1. Outline of figure with indication of garment.

2. Development of the details.

3. Final effect achieved with Indian ink, pen and brush. Note the stylization of the figure and face projecting a young modern image.

3   Fashion detail

It is important when sketching a garment to place all the details in the correct position in relation to the figure in order to achieve the correct balance and proportion of the garment you are illustrating. The shape of a collar, the cut of a sleeve and the placing of pockets, seams, etc., are all relevant.

The fashion artist is concerned with giving an interpretation of a design created by a designer and the drawing should reflect the overall feeling. Observe the details of garments when sketching, making notes on the behaviour of different materials and the way in which they hang and fall into folds. Note also the various styles in sleeves, collars, pleats and pockets. It is good practice to make sketches of them from different angles, keeping the sketches for future reference. It is most useful to study the names of the different styles and effects used in creating a fashion garment, i.e. embroidery, materials, trimmings, sleeves, collars, pleats, etc. This knowledge would be an advantage when reporting a collection.

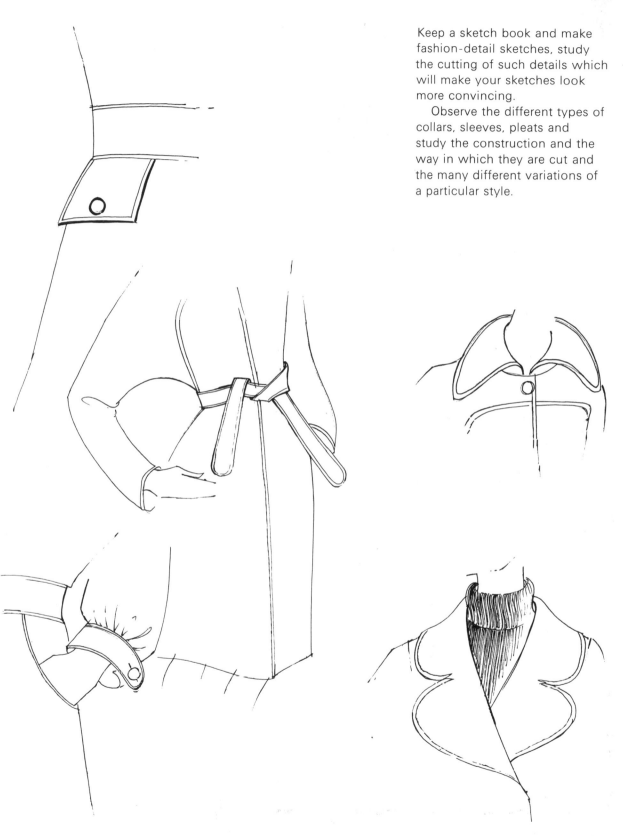

Keep a sketch book and make fashion-detail sketches, study the cutting of such details which will make your sketches look more convincing.

Observe the different types of collars, sleeves, pleats and study the construction and the way in which they are cut and the many different variations of a particular style.

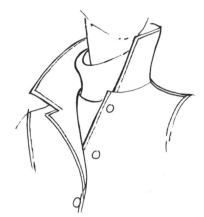

Study the way the collars fit on the neck and the depth of a stand or roll. When sketching it is very easy to give the wrong effect by too much exaggeration in the artist's interpretation.

Make a study of collars, sleeves, pockets and pleats, note the way in which they have been cut and constructed and the many different variations of a particular style. From the basic styles there are many variations.

Note the style details and the effect of the angle of the hat, the tie of a belt. Fashion promotes a different way of wearing clothes and thereby projects an image.

Observe the different types of collars, sleeves, pleats and style details, etc. Study the construction and the way in which they are cut and the many different variations of a particular style.

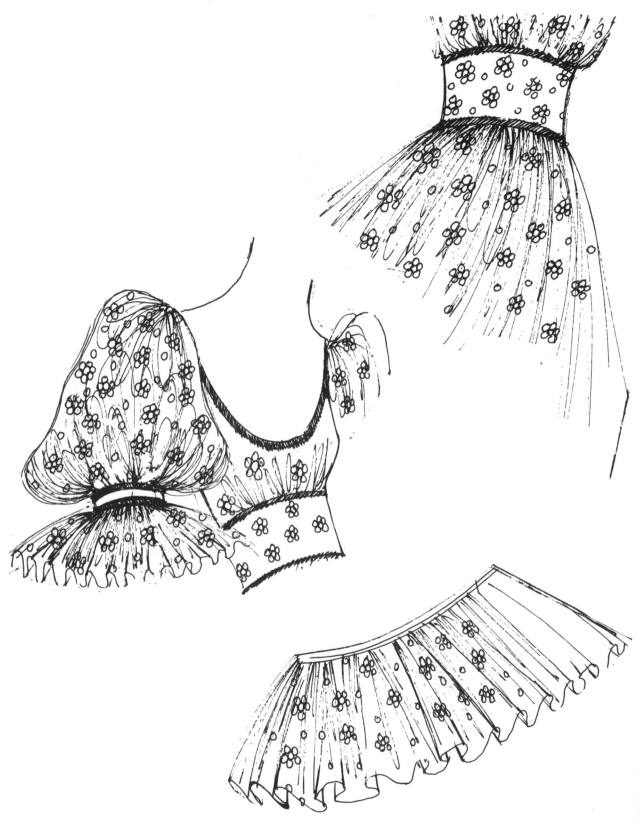

It is useful to make detail sketches studying the way certain effects have been achieved. A designer uses many different techniques to achieve the finished artwork and close observation of, for example, pleating, draping, smocking, quilting or appliqué help in building up a repertoire of effects.

Keep a sketch-book for reference notes, jotting down those points which, when reflected in the drawing, will indicate an understanding of the technical aspects of the clothes being illustrated.

4 Fashion reporting

When reporting for newspapers and magazines, the fashion artist must work with great speed, observing all the main features of a show, the new silhouettes and fashion details. The sketches should reflect the feeling of the show and give an overall impression of the total look projected.

This kind of work requires practice to gain confidence; notes with your sketches will be helpful so when working record details of garments, i.e. colour, fabrics, trimmings, pockets, sleeves, and skirt lengths, etc.

The conditions of working vary considerably. You may not be allowed to sketch when attending a fashion show, and would have to depend on a good memory and observation to express impressions immediately afterwards.

The sketches are usually required as soon as possible. The artist would have little time for experimenting with effects, so it is important to be sure of the style and technique to be used, when making the sketches.

It would be impossible to make a fine detailed sketch in the time and conditions in which the artist invariably works. A quick sketch should be made with brief notes.

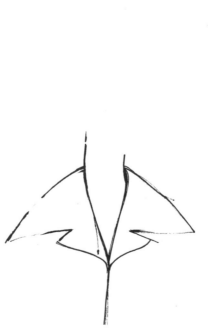

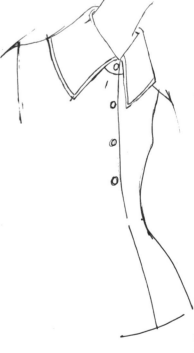

In some instances fashion journalists produce their own drawings together with fashion articles, or they work in conjunction with the artist.

Practise sketching the same detail from different angles. If possible, place a garment on a dressmaker's model and make sketches, observing the appearance from different angles. This exercise will help you gain confidence when working later in a situation when you may be limited in the time in which you are able to view the garment. Practise making quick sketches, observing the main details only.

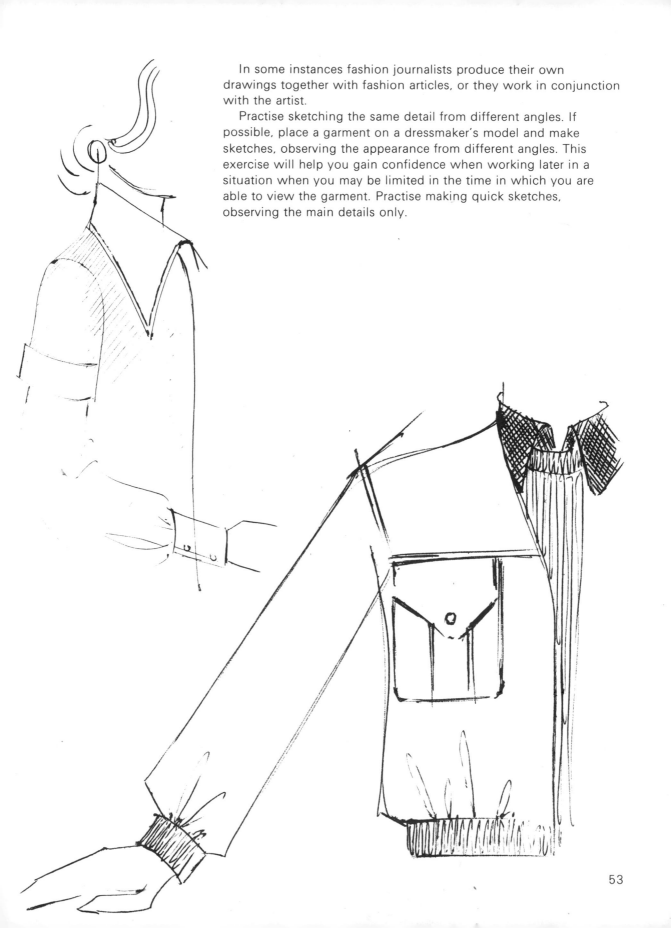

Total look

The overall effect of a fashion is referred to as the 'total look'.

It is important when illustrating a new fashion to observe how the total look has been achieved.

When sketching clothes at a collection the most important things to look for are:

1. *Silhouette* — Cut, shape, texture and surface decoration.

2. *Material* — Colour, weave pattern and texture.

3. *Style Features* — Collars, pockets, sleeves, and outstanding style features.

4. *Theme and Image* — Type of fashion (e.g. elegant, sporty, etc.) and occasion for which the design has been made.

5. *Accessories* — Hats, hair styles, make-up, shoes, stockings, bags and belts, etc.

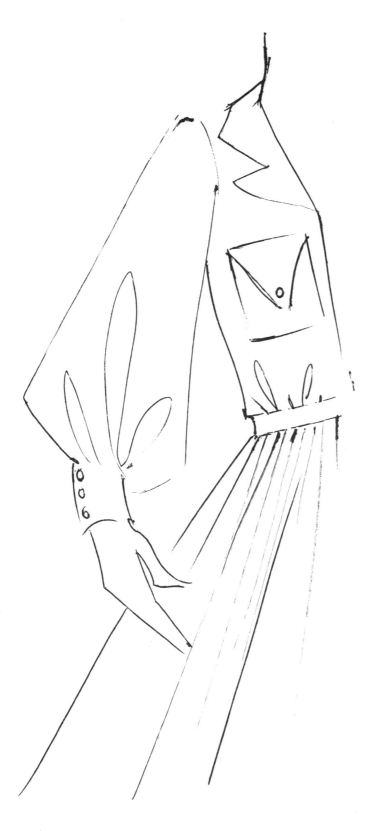

Exercise:

1. Select a garment: a dress, coat or suit.

2. For a limited period (five minutes, no more) study the garment, observing all the main features: cut, shape, texture, collar, sleeves and style features.

3. From memory sketch the garments on figures worked out from imagination and constructed in the way illustrated in Chapter 2.

4. The sketches should be drawn with the effects concentrated on the main impressions.

5. Now compare your sketches with the garments you have been working from. This exercise will help you to gain confidence in observation and speed when working under similar conditions professionally.

Techniques, texture, pattern

Felt-tipped pens have been used for this figure combined with a Rapidograph pen for the finer details.

1. Fibre-point pen.

2. Black Felt pen.

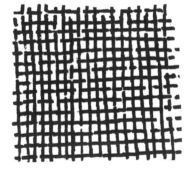

3. Fine brush.

Black pencils and wax crayons

There is a large selection of black pencils on the market ranging from very hard (9H) leads to soft (6B). The following effects have been obtained by using a selection of different papers, combining the surface of the paper with the pencil. It is also possible to create the effect of texture by placing thin paper on a textured surface and by applying a soft pencil to the paper, pieces of textured hardboard. wood, card, metal, etc., many effects may thus be achieved. Note the different movements of the pencil.

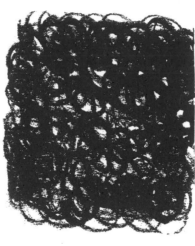

Note the character of a certain material and the way in which the material falls into folds and drapes. Develop methods of depicting the different characteristics of the material without going into great detail. It is often more effective to keep the drawing simple.

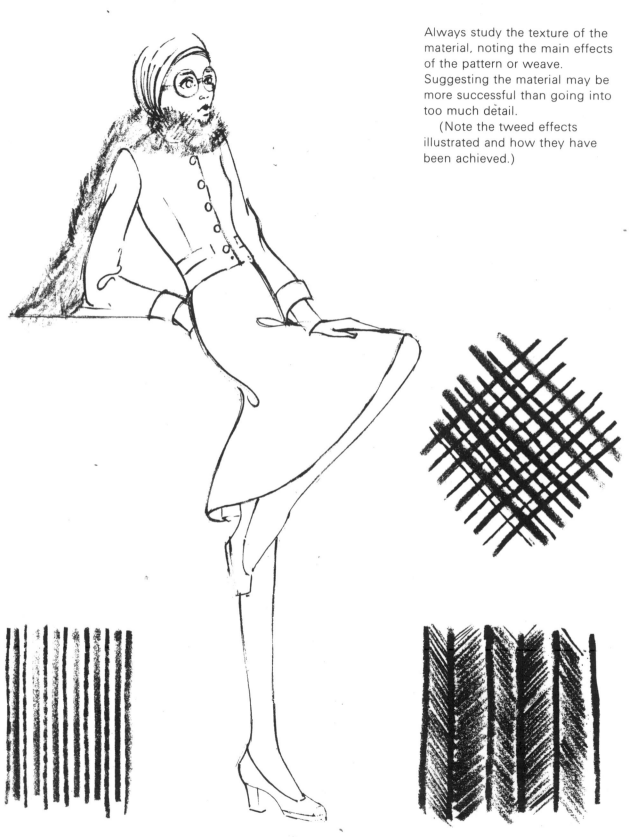

Always study the texture of the material, noting the main effects of the pattern or weave. Suggesting the material may be more successful than going into too much detail.

(Note the tweed effects illustrated and how they have been achieved.)

1. When applying a tone make sure the surface of the paper is clean.

2. Place the tone over the area to be covered and press down lightly.

3. Cut the tone where it is not required and peel sections away.

Illustrated are details from a dress made from a printed chiffon, introducing gathers as a main feature in the design. The chiffon and gathers have been suggested with a fine pen nib and black Indian ink working on a very smooth-surface paper.

Note the way in which the pattern has been used to create a decorative effect.

Letratone combined with fibre-point pen

Letratone has been used for the blouse and tunic to give the effect of texture and pattern. The trousers have been drawn with a fibre-point pen to give the effect of a twill weave. Note the details of the blouse and tunic applied on top of the Letratone surface with pen and waterproof black Indian ink.

Letratone has been used to achieve these effects. There is a large selection of tones and patterns to choose from.

By overlapping the patterns many effects may be achieved. It is also possible to work on the surface of the tone with ink or paint to develop a pattern further. By cutting with a sharp blade or knife it is possible to peel sections away to reveal the paper underneath (see illustrations).

Experiment with different pencils, trying out effects on separate paper before working on the original drawing. By accident you will often discover new effects.

Make a collection of interesting
sample materials of contrasting
texture and pattern.

Study carefully the pattern
and texture and experiment with
a variety of media, to reproduce
an effect of the materials.
Remember that the pattern
would be taken down to scale
to fit the proportion of the figure
and garment being illustrated.

It would not be necessary to
go into great detail unless this
has been requested.

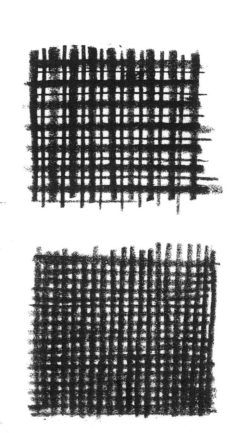

67

Note the characteristics of a certain material and experiment with different pens and pencils until you acquire the desired effects that suggest the material.

Rapidograph pen, fibre-tipped pen combined with black and white ink.

This sketch has been produced using two pens.

The Cardigan: Rapidograph size (5).

Scarf: Fibre-point pen, producing heavy ribbed effect.

Trousers: Tweed herringbone with black Indian ink, applied with brush, combined with fine brush and white ink, working on a smooth-surfaced paper.

(Note the pen and brush movements illustrated.)

This effect of velvet has been achieved with the use of poster paint combined with the white wax of a candle. The wax has been applied first on the parts of the garment to be highlighted, then a wash of paint is added.

Note the different effects made with brush and paint.

Opposite
1. Simple outline sketch with candle wax applied in sections to be highlighted.
2. Black paint applied with large brush to achieve a loose effect.

As an exercise, sketch or trace a figure a number of times, experimenting with different media, i.e. pencils, pen and ink, crayon, pastel, paints, etc. Develop your ideas and techniques of working. You will discover that there are many variations in which to illustrate one idea.

Apply the texture on one side of the garment, leaving the other side to give the effect of light (see page 36). The use of different pressures on the pencil when drawing will give a contrast to the line value.

Exercise:
Sketch or trace a number of figures illustrating the same coat or dress and experiment by producing a variation of tweed effects on each drawing, using black pencils, crayons, and paint, etc.

Production

When preparing art work for reproduction it is useful to have a knowledge and understanding of the techniques. Depending on the printing methods used the artist may have to limit the techniques of the work, according to the costs.

As the work of a fashion artist may vary considerably from illustrations for newspaper articles, magazines, catalogues, to work for exhibitions and window displays, the methods of reproduction vary also.

It is not essential to have a complete technical knowledge of printing as this is a very specialised field, but it is helpful to have a knowledge of the basic principles and the effects achieved, related to costs.

This knowledge would then enable you to discuss your work with agents, art editors and printers with more understanding of the requirements and problems that may arise in connection with the printing cost and techniques to be used. When preparing work for reproduction the main considerations should be:

1. An understanding of the reproduction techniques. This is most important to enable you to produce the correct art work. The type of printing methods being used may narrow the use of line values, tones and the number of colours.

2. The paper on which the work is to be printed may vary considerably.

3. The reduction or enlargement of the work. When work is being 'blown up' for exhibition or display purposes, remember what looks effective drawn on a small scale when enlarged will emphasize certain details and may produce a different effect.

When the work is being reduced the lines should be considered with care as they must be strong enough to take the reduction, if not, some line values could be lost.

Half-tone Wash drawings and photographs must be printed in half-tone. The photo-engraving process reduces the art work to a series of dots of different sizes. The dots are transferred by a photographic process onto the metal plate. The large dots produce the dark tones and the small dots produce the lighter tones. The number of dots to the inch produce the quality of the block and its suitability for printing on different types of paper.

Line block The line block has no half-tones or middle tones. When working on drawings to be produced as line blocks the line value should be well defined. This method is the simplest form of process block consisting of lines on a plain ground.

Fine line work Very fine line drawings require a special treatment and would cost more than the ordinary line block.

Letterpress   A technique of printing in which the inked casts are pressed directly on the paper.

Centre Spread   The opening of a section taken across two pages. The centre opening of a folder where the blocks and type spread across the sheet.

Combination line and half-tone   This type of block is used when a photograph and drawing are combined.

Stipple or mechanical tint   Tints combined with line blocks to provide a background to certain parts of the illustration when it is not possible to produce by hand on the original drawing. A large selection of tints and effects can be produced, using this method.
   Indication is shown as to where the tints are to be used, by shading the appropriate parts with a blue pencil or crayon.

Three- and four-colour process   The half-tone block developed to produce full colour. A different plate is used for each of the primary colours, and these are printed superimposed upon each other.

Offset printing   A method of printing in which the plate covered in ink transfers an impression to a rubber blanket which prints on to the paper.

Typography   Selecting and arranging type for advertisements, magazines, books etc. The art of typography requires a complete understanding of the many different typefaces and spacing.

Proof; engraver's proof   An inked impression of the work for checking and making corrections usually printed on newsprint.

Paste-up   Arranging the art work, type, etc., by pasting the work down before sending it to the printers.

Screen   Used for areas where a half-tone is required.

Bleed   To run blocks off the edge of the paper.

Block   A term used when referring to any kind of line, stereo plate or half-tone used in letterpress printing.

6 Faces, hairstyles and hats

Depending on the type of illustration and image to be projected through your drawing the type of face and expression will vary. Make notes in your sketch book of different types and study the work of other fashion artists.

Make a study of current trends in make-up and hair styles, study magazines, photographs of fashion models and make notes on the techniques of make-up being used, note the colours and effects, i.e. emphasis on eyes and lashes— shape of eyebrows, lips, etc. Remember the current make-up and hair styles are complementary to the clothes worn and the image projected.

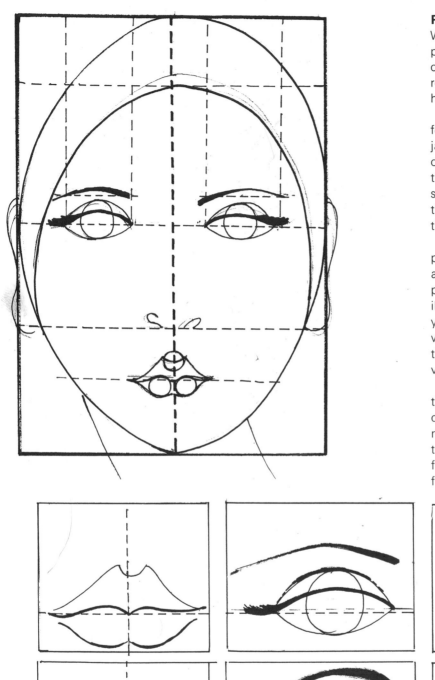

Proportions of the head

When you start drawing heads, practise sketching them on their own, observing the features related to the proportion of the head.

Note the shape of the features, i.e. eyes, nose, mouth, jaw line, cheek bones, etc., observe the different expressions that can be achieved by the shape of the mouth, placing of the eyebrows, and expression in the eyes.

For beginners, it is good practise to sketch the head as an egg shape, working out the proportions of the features as illustrated. By using this method you will develop a technique which will help you in turning the head profile—three-quarter view or full-face.

Once you have developed this method of arriving at the correct proportions you should now practice different techniques of drawing the features to achieve different facial expressions.

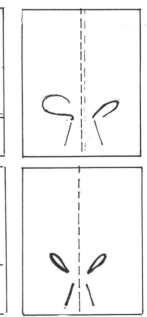

Note the curved line following the egg shape of the head. When starting a sketch of the head note the following stages:

1. Sketch the oval shape of the head.

2. Work out the proportions of the placement of the features as illustrated.

3. Outline the hair line creating a style round the head.

4. Develop the make-up depending on the effects required.

Study the details of a hair style, noting the effects.

Experiment with different materials to achieve the effects required. With constant practice you will discover the media to give the correct effect.

The type of paper and surface are important, a large selection of different quality papers with different surfaces are available.

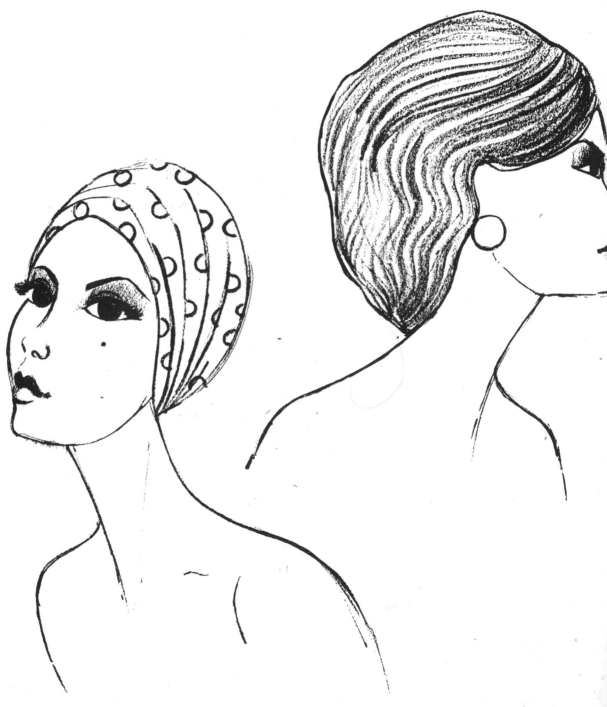

Profile

Create the profile within a square box, with the chin placed in one corner as illustrated. The features would then be placed using the balance lines.

Practise sketching different fashion types. Imagine a certain Image, i.e. Classic, Sophisticated, Casual, Exotic, etc., and try sketching the head and correct hair style from imagination. This will help you to gain confidence when working without reference.

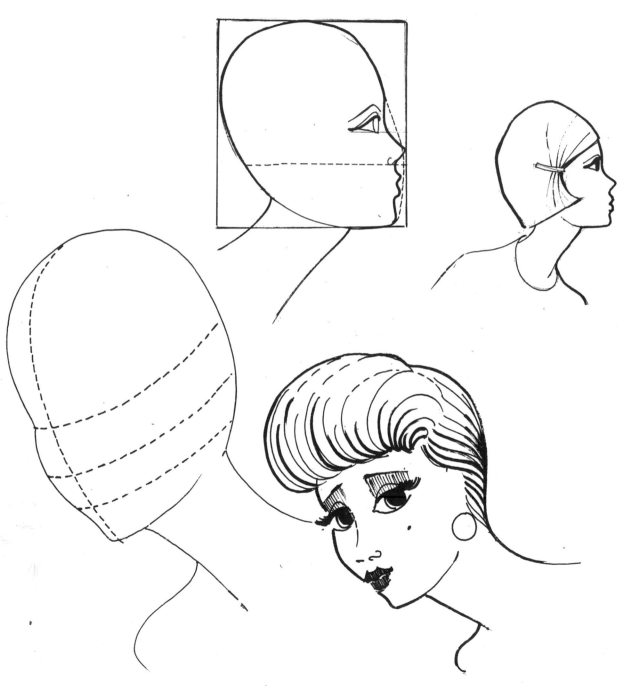

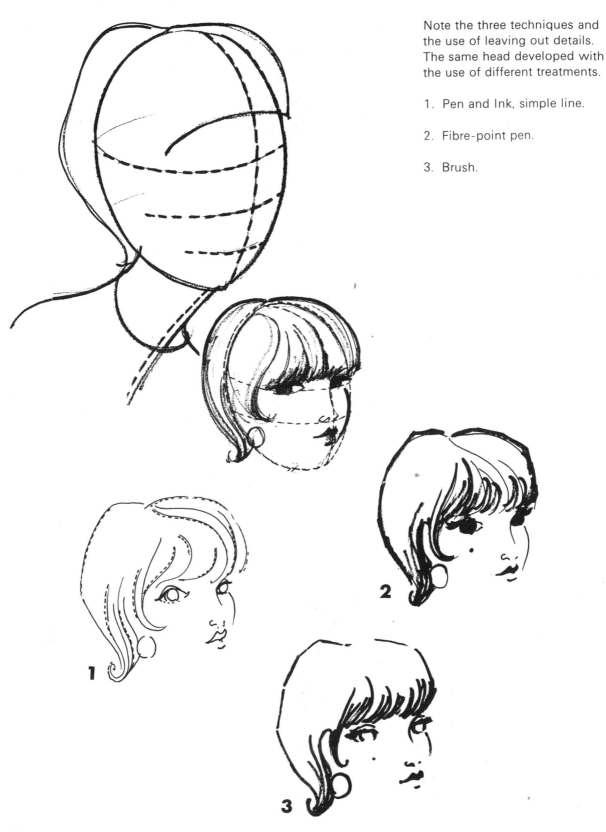

Note the three techniques and the use of leaving out details. The same head developed with the use of different treatments.

1. Pen and Ink, simple line.

2. Fibre-point pen.

3. Brush.

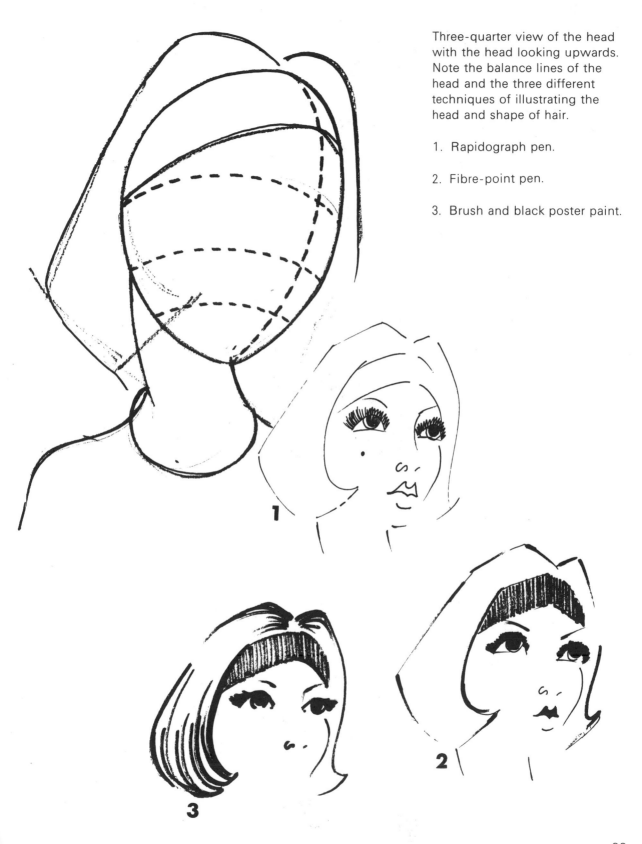

Three-quarter view of the head with the head looking upwards. Note the balance lines of the head and the three different techniques of illustrating the head and shape of hair.

1. Rapidograph pen.

2. Fibre-point pen.

3. Brush and black poster paint.

Hair styles

Hair styles change with fashion trends—the shape, outline of the hair style is part of a total look.

The hair style is very important when illustrating a fashion. It should be balanced and in keeping with the design you are illustrating and image you wish to project.

Styles are changing all the time, the fashion artist must observe new fashion trends in hair styles, studying new styles at fashion shows, noting different shapes, cut and colour. Wigs and hair pieces have now become very fashionable. This enables women to change the hair fashions to achieve a total look.

The history of hair dressing is a useful subject to study. The Fashion designer is constantly using historical research for inspiration.

When illustrating a fashion it is not always necessary to go into great detail unless the illustration demands this. The artist should observe line and direction of the hair, general effects, texture and styling need only be suggested.

Fibre-point pens have been used to achieve the illustrated effects. A large selection of pens of this type with different size points are available. Collect a selection and experiment with different sizes combined in the one sketch.

Hats

When illustrating hats it is important to sketch the type of face and hair style to complement the hat, i.e. Casual, Elegant, Sophisticated.

Make sure the hat fits the head and is sketched at the correct angle showing it to full advantage. Use balance lines as illustrated for the correct effect.

It is advisable to make some preliminary rough sketches before deciding on the final sketch to be developed.

Exercise:

1. Select a collection of hats as varied as possible. Working from a live model, if you are not able to arrange this use a milliner's block.

2. Sketch the hat from different angles, this will enable you to make a selection and decide on the most attractive features illustrating the hat to its full advantage.

3. Now trace the selected sketch four times and experiment with different techniques, using pen and ink, brush, fibre-point pen and pen and wash.

7 Fashion images

The mood or feeling of a particular fashion can be suggested by the pose and attitude of the figure on which you are illustrating the garment. The technique used has a strong influence on the feeling which the illustration will project. It is helpful to study the work of fashion artists and the many techniques used by them during different periods and to observe how the various periods reflect their own style and presentation. During the past years the layout and styles of work have been influenced by Art Nouveau, Art Deco., Pop Art and a feeling of the Twenties, Thirties and Forties. Hollywood and film personalities have also had an impact. The images of Carmen Miranda, Jean Harlow, Rita Hayworth and many other stars of Hollywood and the film industry have been used as a theme for inspiration by designers.

Make a study of graphic work produced during the different periods. Books on the history of fashion and graphic design, old collections of magazines and fashion plates are all useful for study. On visits to costume museums, make sketches of the different costumes from the periods displayed and study the details of a sleeve, the cut of a collar or the drape of a skirt. All this will help in the development of observing detail.

It is helpful to keep a collection of fashion illustrations and photographs that appeal to you for future reference when making a study of style and techniques. The collection should be kept in separate files under different headings, e.g. Coats, Evening Wear, Children's and Sports, etc.

Study the work of different artists and note the detail of the drawings and paintings of the figures and clothes worn. The work of Holbein, Watteau, Boucher and Ingres, to name a few, will all provide technical inspiration.

The posters by such artists as Toulouse-Lautrec, Steinlein, Mucha and Dudovich and fashion illustrations by Erté, R. R. Bouche, and other artists of more recent times will be similarly helpful.

Keep in touch with new fashions in sport, music, dancing and entertainment, for these are the activities that are influencing fashion and making new demands on the designer. A fashion, or a period, projected through a new film, play or musical, worn by a personality may create a new fashion given the right publicity. A sport that has suddenly become fashionable will create a demand for clothes to complement the activity. This consideration may also apply to travel and new ways of spending holidays, new trends in dancing and all aspects of social entertainment.

Fashion images vary considerably depending on the occasion and the type of person wearing a particular fashion. Some artists specialize in portraying a certain type, e.g. Sporty, Sophisticated, Young, etc.

When developing and working on ideas for a pose to illustrate the garment to its best advantage, imagine the figure in movement, walking, turning, etc. Start by making a selection of rough sketches of the figure, decide on the most suitable pose you consider to reflect the right feeling or mood of the garment (see illustrations).

It is good practice to make notes on what makes a certain fashion image; how the effect has been achieved. Through study of the reports of fashion journalists writing for newspapers and magazines the artist may keep constantly in tune with the current development.

Elegant and casual

Final sketch using pen and ink technique combined with Letratone. Chinese White paint has been used to highlight the eyes and the beads and buttons on the dress.

A dark tone has been used to provide a sun-tanned effect and to give contrast to the black-and-white spotted cotton dress. Note the emphasis on the large puff-sleeves and small waist effect. The style being simple, the head and hair style has been developed, and beads have been introduced to add interest and to give the drawing movement.

If a design is elaborate and detailed it is usually more effective to keep the hair style and face to a simple line technique in order not to overpower the effect of the garment.

The image projected through the drawing is casual and elegant. The effect of the soft camel-hair coat has been achieved with a very dry fibre-point pen. The pose is relaxed.

Layout and presentation

The presentation of your work should be considered with care; when producing a drawing the size of reproduction and the space allotted are vital considerations.

Note the use of colour leaving a white line to reveal the details of the coat.

The simple background provides the figure with atmosphere and added dimension.

When working for a magazine, newspaper or studio the artist would be directed and given advice as to the style of drawing required and in what context it would be used. The artist might have been given the job because of a particular style.

As there are different methods in the reproduction of art work, it is an advantage to have an understanding of production techniques.

Presenting the work

Presentation of your work is very important when showing it to an agent, art director or buyer.

Be selective in the work you take for an interview; it should be arranged so that it is easy to handle with a varied selection reflecting your own style. Discard the drawings with which you are not satisfied and redraw. Never take too many, a small collection of a high standard is more impressive.

You will find a large range of portfolios in different sizes in any good artist's materials shop. Books with transparent envelopes in which to protect and display your work are also effective. Work mounted on thin card is of advantage if it is to be handled continually, with a protective cover of tracing paper or thin sheet of acetate.

It may be more convenient in some instances to have your work photographed and taken down to a smaller scale. If possible it is helpful to mount all your work the same size, as this makes it easy to handle a collection of drawings. The size of the work varies according to the artist and style. Most art directors and editors prefer 'half a size up'.

It is useful to date your work for reference.

Agents

The fashion artist may work through an agent, should the agent consider the work suitable. When working through an agent a percentage will be deducted from your fee. Apart from being able to advise you the agent has the experience which should help him in placing your work.

Commercial studios

Working full-time in a commercial studio is excellent experience, especially for the student leaving college. The work would be varied and provide an insight into the world of commercial art.

Stores

Departmental stores have studios in their advertising and display departments, some employ fashion artists full-time, but most use freelance fashion artists.

Preparation of work for reproduction

When producing work for reproduction the work would be designed to fit into the space or shape allotted. It is best to make the drawing half a size larger than the size it is to be reproduced (see illustrations). Some artists, however, work on a large scale, in which case the drawing would be taken down to the size required. Illustration shown prepared for reproduction, and when taken down in size. The sketch has been reduced by half.

1. Black and white stylised drawing illustrating two figures projecting a young modern image in casual winter trouser suits accessorised with knitted hats and scarves to give the outfit added interest.

2. When preparing a colour overlay for reproduction the transparent film would be placed over the line drawing and paint applied to indicate the areas of colour. Stage two shows the overlay separated from the sketch.

3. Drawing as reproduced in colour.

Note the reduction of the drawing illustrated. When working for a particular commission you should enquire about the size of the work when reduced; this is important when using fine line values as they could be lost if taken down to a small scale.

Sketch from life and attend life classes whenever possible. Adapt from your sketches experimenting with line, pattern and texture. Many effects may be achieved from the original idea. If a model should not be available select some good photographs from fashion magazines.

The use of a decorative frame may also give a pleasing effect to the fashion sketch suggesting a feeling or period to complement the design being illustrated, i.e. evening wear, sports wear or children's clothes.

The study of decorative prints—flower studies and paintings—will be useful when designing and selecting the correct decoration for a particular drawing.

Remember the border or background sketch is being used to give atmosphere and complement the design, therefore care should be taken not to overpower the fashion illustrated.

A simple background sketch will give a fashion drawing added interest.

Presentation
Note how a simple line has been used to create interest in combination with the illustration of the figure.

Note the different arrangements of the same figures arranged within a frame, and the use of a solid black panel.

Showing the stages of a two-colour illustration. The figures have been cut out and mounted on a grey paper with a simple background in line to give atmosphere and depth. The transparent overlay has been placed on top of the figures indicating the pattern of the fabric breaking the pattern to give the effect of light falling on the dresses.

1. Simple line frame produced with a thin black adhesive tape, combined with a solid black shape against which the figure has been displayed.

2. Black circle with figure placed to one side, creating a very simple but pleasing effect.

3. Black and white panels and thin white tape was used to achieve this effect.

Exercise:
Cut out a selection of shapes in black and white thin card or paper, create a selection of backgrounds, then place your fashion sketches against the backgrounds, experimenting with different arrangements.

Presenting a figure against a panel. Note the effects achieved with the introduction of a simple frame.

The introduction of solid combined with the illustration makes a black background interesting contrast.
Note the white lines framing the sketch produced by applying a thin white tape.

When experimenting with the arrangement of figures it is useful to make roughs of the different garments you are illustrating, then cut them out and place them in different positions, until you achieve the effect required (see illustrations). When you have decided on the arrangement you think most effective you paste the roughs down. The original work would then be made, using the layout as a guide.

Men's fashion

Men's fashion is an important section of the clothing industry. New designs for formal and informal wear have developed over the past years with the introduction of many new styles from different parts of the world.

Men's fashions have been promoted through boutiques, fashion magazines, newspaper articles and fashion shows.

Designers are now specialising in this area. The selection of fabrics, patterns and textures are very varied and offer a source of inspiration to the designer.

When illustrating men's wear the artist should consider:

1. The type of garment to be illustrated and the most attractive angle to present it.

2. The 'image' to be projected, i.e. face, hairstyle, stance, etc.

3. The treatment of the illustration to create the correct environment to sell the design, e.g. pen and ink, brush, wash, etc.

4. How the drawing is to be used in relation to the advertisement for the newspaper, magazine, catalogue, etc., and the printing methods used.

Sketch illustrating men's wear. Study with care the cut and details, make sure the garment really fits the figure. Note how the tweed patterns have been suggested and the indication of the way the material has been cut.

117

Three arrangements of the same sketch.

Note the use of a simple line to add interest.

1. Two horizontal lines.

2. Frame with the figure placed off centre.

Glossary

Advertising Manager

Responsible for the organization of the department creating advertisements for newspapers and all aspects of advertising. The staff varies depending on the size of the magazine, advertising agency or store.

The department usually consists of:
Advertising manager (director)
Copy writers
Illustrators
Lay-out artist
Production staff

Within a store the department usually works together with the fashion buyers or fashion co-ordinators and display manager. The work involves arranging special sales promotions, fashion shows, exhibitions, etc.

Display Manager

Responsible for window displays, interior, exhibitions, fashion shows and special promotions. Works together with advertising department and buyers. The display department would consist of display manager, assistant display manager, window dressers, studio staff, carpenters, electricians, ticket writers, etc. This would depend on the size of the store.

Fashion Buyer
The buyer is responsible for selecting merchandise for a department and may be in charge of one department or more. Must have a complete understanding of fashion and the store's policy.

Copy Writer
The copy writer creates the text for advertisements and articles for newspapers and magazines using information obtained from buyers and manufacturers. The work requires imagination and originality.

Copy
The text of the article or advertisement.

Colour Overlay
The colour overlay is a sheet of transparent paper placed over the illustration to indicate the use of colour.

Clippings
A collection of advertisements and photographs from magazines, newspapers, etc. used for reference. This collection can be most useful when studying the work of other layout and fashion artists.

Blow-up
This term is used when having the work enlarged.

Cropping
To trim the art-work or photographs to fit into a space allocated.

Materials

Fashion boards   High quality board extra thick will take charcoal, crayon, gouache, tempera and water-colour paints.

Water-colour boards   Saunders Water Colour Boards prepared from a mould-made paper. The paper has an even surface.

Bristol board   The board has a high rag content with a fine white surface. Ideal for pen and ink work.

Pasteboard   An inexpensive white board for paste-up and general studio use.

Illustration boards   A board with a smooth surface which will take ink, crayon, pencil, wash or colour. Produced in different sizes.

Cartridge paper   White paper with a finely grained surface suitable for pencil, crayon and colour. This paper is made in different thicknesses and quality.

Coloured cartridge paper   The surface has a slight texture. Suitable for colour work Will take water colour and pastels.

Cartridge pads   Obtainable in a range of sizes with a stiff cardboard back.

Lay-out pads   White lay-out detail paper with a surface ideal for ink and pencil. Usually glued at top to strong cardboard back. Available in different sizes.

Ingres paper   The surface of this paper is ideal for pastel and tempera work. Good selection of colours.

Coloured tissue papers   Unglazed tissue paper, available in a large range of colours, is used in studios to produce inexpensive colour effects. The paper can be stuck to board or paper surfaces with Cow gum or adhesive spray.

Tracing paper and pads   Obtainable in sheets of different sizes or pads.

Herculene tracing film   Polyester film of good quality. Will take pencil and ink, ideal for photo copying, also colour separation work. May also be used for the protection of visual work.

Permatrace   Film with excellent drawing surface for ink and pencil. This film is virtually indestructible.

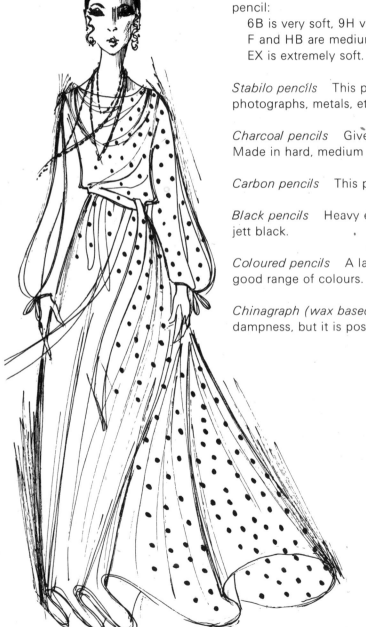

Tracing cloth   Good quality tracing cloth for work that must withstand considerable handling and wear.

Detail paper   A white paper with a high degree of transparency. suitable when working from original roughs.

Pencils
A large selection of pencils is obtainable; the type of pencil used would depend on the effect required.

Pencils (Wood cased)   The degree of hardness is printed on each pencil:
  6B is very soft, 9H very hard
  F and HB are medium
  EX is extremely soft.

Stabilo pencils   This pencil will write on any surface: film, glossy photographs, metals, etc.

Charcoal pencils   Gives the same effect as pure charcoal sticks. Made in hard, medium or soft qualities.

Carbon pencils   This pencil will produce a dull matt finish.

Black pencils   Heavy extra large leads for bold drawings in matt jett black.

Coloured pencils   A large variety of makes is available with a good range of colours.

Chinagraph (wax based)   This pencil is impervious to water and dampness, but it is possible to remove with a dry cloth.

Pens

A large selection of pens is available; listed are some chosen for the different effects that may be achieved.

Rapidograph pens   Technical pens that provide a means of drawing without the aid of constant refilling. The drawing point may be replaced with different sizes. Many pleasing effects may be obtained with the use of this pen, and also in combination with others (see illustrations page 47).

Osmiroid fountain pens   A pen for lettering and script writing. A large range of interchangeable screw-in nibs (not suitable with Indian ink).

Technos drawing pen   The Pelikan Technos is a cartridge-filled drawing pen. Pen points are designed for different jobs, e.g. ruling, stencilling, and free hand. Many interchangeable points are available.

Osmiroid Sketch fountain pen   A very versatile sketching pen which provides a wide variety of line thickness from bold to a fine outline. This pen is fitted with a reservoir to maintain a constant ink flow. Indian ink should not be used.

Pen holders   Many very simple wood or plastic pen holders with nibs are obtainable at a small cost.

A large selection of paints of varying qualities are manufactured:
  Watercolours
  Designer Colours
  Poster Paints
  Tubes of Oil Paint.

Pastels   Pastels vary depending on the quality.

Coloured inks   A large selection of coloured inks are available, some of which are waterproof.

Brushes   Brushes are made in many sizes and qualities (sable, hog and squirrel hair).

Transparent acetate sheet   Cellulose acetate film. Suitable for covering art work and presentation.

Presentation books   Fitted with clear acetate pockets, ideal for presentation of work—photographs, drawings, etc.

Portfolios   Strong durable portfolios in different sizes for storing art work.

Leathercloth portfolios   Ideal for the protection of art work and carrying. Fitted with handle, two fasteners and a centre lock and key. Made in different sizes.

Stanley knife   A craft knife with replaceable blades, ideal for cutting thick paper, heavy card, plastics, etc.

Swivel-head knives   Cuts irregular curves, may be locked for straight lines.

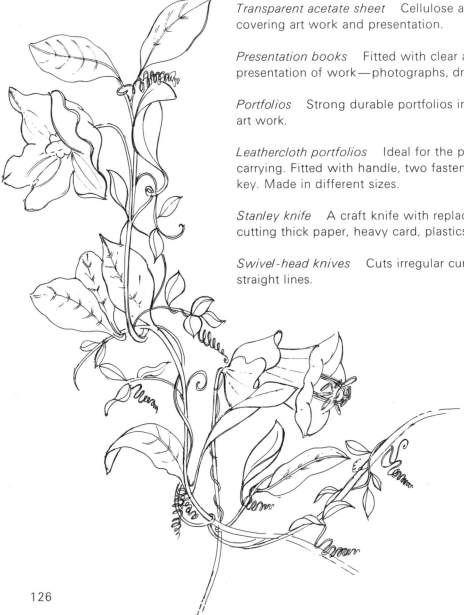

Double-sided adhesive tape   Suitable for quick mounting. Adhesive on both sides.

Protective sprays   Spray to protect art work against damage— obtainable in gloss or matt.

Adhesive in aerosol cans   Spray adhesive—colourless and water repellant. Will stick cloth, board, paper.

Cow gum   Transparent rubber solution suitable for pasting work up. Sold in tins or tubes.

Copydex   Very strong latex adhesive, may be used with paper and fabric.

Gum eraser or paper cleaner   A soft pliable eraser gum. Suitable for cleaning Art work. Will not damage the surface of the paper.

Kneaded eraser   A putty rubber that can be moulded to the shape required.

Staedtler Mars plastic   For use on drafting film, tracing cloth or paper.

Soft eraser   A white soft eraser for soft lead.

Masking tape   Tape seals with light pressure, with a water repellant back.

Drafting tape   Designed to hold film or paper to a drawing board and removed without damage. A very thin, adhesive crepe paper tape.

Light box   A box with a glass top containing a light, used for tracing. By placing the work to be traced on a piece of transparent paper which lays on the glass and is illuminated underneath by the light the work is thrown into clear outline. These boxes are available in a range of sizes or can be quite easily constructed with even the most rudimentary knowledge of carpentry.

Editor's shears   Paper shears with sharp point.

Drawing boards   Lamps with an adjustable arm that concentrates the light in the position required, can be clamped to the board or free-standing.

Transpaseal   Flexible sheet of thin transparent plastic coated with a pressure-sensitive adhesive, obtainable in clear gloss or matt finish. Suitable for covering art work.

Drawing stands   A varied selection are available made of wood and metal, in different sizes. The board can be adjusted according to the angle required.

Plan chest   A chest designed to store drawings and large sheets of paper and card. Available in different units of drawers and sizes.

Air brush   The air brush provides perfectly even tones, graded tints and soft lines, also the blending of colours. Operated by a motor compressor or compressed air propellant aerosols.